How to Invest in Real Estate for Beginners

Flipping Houses and Rental Property Investing

By D.K. Livingston

Text Copyright © 2019 D.K. Livingston

All Rights Reserved

No part of this book may be reproduced

in any way without the written

permission of the author.

Disclaimer:

The views expressed within this book are those of the author alone. The information contained within this book is based on the opinions, experiences, and observations of the author and is provided "AS-IS". No warranties of any kind are made. Neither the author nor publisher are engaged in rendering professional services of any kind. Neither the author nor publisher will assume liability or responsibility for any loss or damage related directly or indirectly to the information contained within this book.

The author has attempted to be as accurate as possible with the information contained within this book. Neither the author nor publisher will assume responsibility or liability for any errors, omissions, inconsistencies, or inaccuracies.

Table of Contents

Introduction 1
Pros and Cons to Different Types of Real Estate Investments 3
Flipping Real Estate 3
Buying and Holding 5
Renting out Property 6
Real Estate Investment Trusts (REITs) 6
How to Raise Capital to Purchase Real Estate 8
How to Identify Good Real Estate Investment Opportunities 12
Location 12
Property 14
Types of Property Upgrades that Produce the Biggest Returns 16
How to Make an Offer on a Property 20
How to Select Potentially Good Tenants 22
How to Make Real Estate Investing More Passive 24
How to Invest in Real Estate without Having to Manage Tenants, Hire Property Managers, or Maintain Physical Property 27
Closing 34
More from D.K. Livingston 35

Introduction

Purchasing real estate can be a lucrative investment strategy, as well as a great way to generate passive income.

Real estate investing has been around for thousands of years, so we could say that it has withstood the test of time.

It is generally less volatile than stocks and bonds, which makes it more predictable.

Whether the condition of the overall market is up or down, there is potential for profit.

Like all businesses, it has its challenges, but it also has very appealing benefits that can certainly make it worth while.

If done correctly, the benefits can be maximized to their fullest potential.

It's possible to buy certain properties for a low percentage down payment, which makes startup costs relatively low.

Success as a real estate investor typically involves buying the right properties in the right places at the right times. But there is more to it than that.

There's a variety of different property investment options available, including:

- Single family houses

- Small multifamily properties

- Large multifamily properties

- Mobile homes

- Land

- REIT

Part of being a successful real estate investor is having the ability to identify potential profit-making opportunities when others only seem to see problems.

But you need to know which problems are worth fixing, so that you can get a return on your investment.

Whether you'd like to flip houses or buy properties for the purpose of renting them out, this book can help.

It will cover:

- **Pros and cons to different types of real estate investments**

- **How to raise capital to purchase real estate**

- **How to identify good real estate investment opportunities**

- **Types of property upgrades that produce the biggest returns**

- **How to make an offer on a property**

- **How to select potentially good tenants**

- **How to make real estate investing more passive**

- **and more**

__Pros and Cons to Different Types of Real Estate Investments__

When it comes to investing in real estate, the variety of available options might feel a bit overwhelming.

How should investors know which method is best for them?

All of the methods have the potential to generate profits. But some investors might find it easier to generate profits by flipping houses, while other investors might prefer to buy an apartment building and rent out the units.

Looking at the pros and cons of the different types of real estate investments can help you make an informed decision about which route to take.

Flipping Real Estate

Flipping real estate is the process of buying a property with the intention of selling it for profit at a later time, similar to the way a stock market trader would buy a stock with the intention of selling it after the share price goes up.

This type of real estate investment plan often involves buying a property that is in need of repair. The investor will typically hire people to fix anything that needs to be repaired, and then put the property up for sale after the necessary repairs are complete.

Sometimes even if if the property does not need repairs, it could still benefit from renovation. The investor might see a property as an outdated diamond in the rough that could use a modernized look, and then decide to have it renovated.

Property flipping is the process of flipping properties regularly, instead of buying property and holding onto it for several years and hoping that it will appreciate.

Pros:

• Flipping properties regularly can provide quicker returns than buying and holding a single property long-term. In this case, it is comparable to trading stocks regularly in the stock market, rather than buying just one and holding onto it for several years. The long series of short-term gains can add up quicker.

• Flipping properties on a regular basis can help the investor gain experience fairly quick. If an investor puts big money into one large property and waits for it to appreciate over several years, and then it loses value, that could mean it took the investor several years to learn one lesson. But if an investor is flipping a property every three to four months, and the property investment loses value, that investor can learn from his or her mistake in twelve to sixteen weeks and move on.

• If repair or renovation is involved, it can provide a feeling of satisfaction for transforming a mundane property into an excellent one.

• Since there will be no tenants, the investor will not have to deal with having to check up on them.

Cons:

• The potential for quicker returns also brings the risk of quicker losses, which can accumulate just as fast.

• There are "property flipping" rules in place that could cause conflict when the investor tries to sell the property.

• The transaction costs involved with buying and selling can add up quicker.

- It can be considered somewhat more active than passive because the investor has to keep finding new properties to fix up and sell.

Buying and Holding

If property flipping is similar to trading stocks on a shorter time frame, then buying and holding property is similar to a long-term investment in the stock market.

Pros:

- Since buying and holding takes more time than quick flips, transaction fees associated with constant buying and selling will be lower.

- It can be considered somewhat more passive than quick flipping, because if done correctly, the investor can simply wait for the property to appreciate.

- The property can be rented out to tenants while the investor waits for it to increase in value.

- Since the long-term investors are in it for the long run, they don't have to constantly analyze every small change that occurs in the market.

Cons:

- Buying and holding onto a property for several years or more can cause property taxes to accumulate significantly.

- Maintenance will often need to be done regularly to make sure that the property value holds, and those costs can reduce profits.

- It can take the real estate market a while to recover if it is in a downtrend, which can require tremendous patience.

- Unless the investor is renting out the property to tenants, it can take several years or more before any profit from the property is realized.

Renting out Property

If you have the patience to manage tenants, renting out property might be for you.

Pros:

• Instead of simply waiting for a property to increase in value, the investor has the added benefit of generating income from tenants in the meantime.

• Management can be outsourced.

Cons:

• Although it's a worst-case scenario, tenants can damage property.

• Vacancies can disrupt the cash flow process.

Real Estate Investment Trusts (REITs)

This is an alternative to investing in real estate the traditional way. REITs are basically stocks, so instead of purchasing property, shares are bought by the investor. A REIT doesn't acquire real estate properties for the purpose of reselling them, but instead, to keep them for its own operations.

Pros:

• Since it's a stock, everything can be done digitally, instead of having to acquire a physical piece of property. When it's time to cash out, there is no need for a realtor or title transfer.

• Dividends are offered.

• The open exchange-traded REITs offer higher liquidity.

Cons:

- Less control.

How to Raise Capital to Purchase Real Estate

If you are looking to buy real estate with little money down, there are financing options available that allow you to do so.

This chapter will cover some of the different options that real estate investors have to raise capital for their purchases.

Adjustable-Rate Mortgage

This is also known as a floating-rate mortgage. With this type of mortgage, the interest rate is adjustable. Typically, the initial interest rate will be fixed for a certain time period, and then it will get reset on an annual or monthly basis.

The adjustment is based on an index that mirrors the cost to the lender of borrowing on the credit markets.

Oftentimes, Adjustable-Rate Mortgages will have a limit as to how high the rate can go or a cap rate as to how much the interest rate can change from year to year.

Pros:

• The bank will often give you the gift of a lower initial rate. This is possibly done to help balance out the risk of having the rates move up later on. A lower initial rate can be particularly beneficial if you are interested in short-term financing, because by the time the rates move up significantly, the financing process could be out of the way already.

• The interest rate might decrease later on.

Cons:

- Unpredictability

- Fairly complex

Conventional Loan

Many borrowers can get conventional loans from a bank for only 20%, but that's under the assumption that the borrower will be using the property as their primary residence. Investors might need to put down approximately 30%.

Pros:

- Fairly straight forward and less complex

- Very common, so it's highly available

- Low interest rates compared to many other types of loans

Cons:

- It can take approximately a month to get one

- There is a limit that dictates how many conventional loans you can have

- Substantial down payment is required for investors

Federal Housing Administration Loans

FHA loans are sponsored by the government. They give the borrower the option of only having to put a small amount of money down.

Depending on what your credit score is, the down payment could be as low as 3.5%. A FICO score between 500 and 579 will get you a 10% down payment. A FICO score of 580 or higher will secure a 3.5% down payment.

The title of the property must be in your name.

Pros:

• Low down payment

• Credit score doesn't have to be excellent.

• Fairly low interest rate

Cons:

• You must live at the residence for at least a year

• Stricter appraisal and inspection requirements

• Mortgage insurance is required, which will add to the costs

Hard Money

Hard Money loans are short-term loans that are typically borrowed from private investors or a company.

The interest rates for this type of loan are usually rather high (10% to 18%), due to the shorter duration and increased risk factor.

When a real estate investor is looking for a quick loan, and the more traditional options have not worked out, a Hard Money loan can be considered.

Instead of focusing on your debt to income ratio, like many traditional lenders do, the Hard Money lenders primarily focus on collateral. If you can't repay the loan, they take the house that was used as collateral and try to sell it.

Pros:

• It's flexible, and therefore, easier to qualify for

• It's fast

- Offer up to 70% APR

Cons:

- High interest rates

- Since these types of loans are short-term, you might not have enough time to pay it back

- Closing fees and origination fees can be high

Home Equity Line of Credit

This can be used if you have bought a home already and have equity attached to it. It gives the person a revolving credit line as a result of the line of credit being secured by the home.

To illustrate, if a person owns a house that is worth $1,000,000, and half of it has already been paid off, the lender might give that person $500,000 as a line of credit. The loan allows the person to use the $500,000 worth of equity to purchase another property.

Pros:

- Often has a lower interest rate than other popular loan types

- Interest may be tax deductible

Cons:

- Since your home is being used as collateral, the lender is allowed to foreclose if payments are not made on time

- For most people, the biggest asset they own will be their home. But since this type of loan is forcing them to spend equity in their home, their main asset can be depleted.

How to Identify Good Real Estate Investment Opportunities

Having the ability to identify opportunities is a very important part of being a real estate investor.

Some problems can be profitable when improved upon, while others will reduce profits by more than what the trouble is worth.

For example, putting a large amount of money into a fixer-upper will not be worth it if you don't get a return on your investment.

As you begin your real estate market analysis for potential opportunities, a good place to start is with location.

Location

When selecting a location for a property to invest in, realize that things can get more complicated if the place is located out of state, out of province, etc.

Even if you hire property management, you will still probably want to make occasional trips to your investment property in order to see for yourself that the property managers and tenants are telling you the truth about what is going on.

Money can be another potential concern.

Long distance means more time and traveling costs spent to get there.

The further away it is, the more tempted you might be to not go over there to look things over.

For this reason, it might be easier to start out with neighborhoods that are within a somewhat comfortable distance of your primary residence.

When selecting a location for your real estate investment, it's important to make sure that it meets a certain criteria.

• **Convenience:** Generally, properties that are located near shopping malls, major stores, and train stations will present better opportunities for selling.

• **Economics:** Ideally, potential clients should have high-paying jobs in the area you are selling the property in.

Of course, most people with the highest-paying jobs live in the most expensive areas, and most investors cannot afford to purchase multi-million dollar properties.

Look into middle class areas where the unemployment rate is low. Try to find an area where the median salary is not below the national average.

To obtain information about jobless rates, average hourly earnings, and other economic information, visit:

https://www.bls.gov/

• **Expansion:** If a town that you are interested in buying property in is not known for its ideal location, make sure that it is at least showing signs of expansion.

If new businesses have been opening in a town, or if a major retail chain has selected the area for one of its stores, that could be a sign that the economy in that area might start to change for the better.

•**Laws:** Certain cities might have regulations in place that limit the amount of money you can rent a unit for. Pay attention to rental laws, eviction laws, and property taxes.

• **Population:** Population growth or the lack thereof is another thing to consider. This one speaks volumes for itself.

If people are leaving or going to a particular area in droves, it is usually for a reason. Typically, the denser the population, the higher the demand for places to live.

• **Safety:** Crime rates are definitely something to take into consideration when investing in a property.

Even if you find tenants for a property in a high-crime neighborhood, there is still a greater risk of stolen merchandise, vandalism, etc.

When visiting the neighborhood, look out for warning signs, such as, barred windows, cashiers standing behind bars or a plate of glass at places of business, etc.

For crime statistics, visit:

http://www.city-data.com/crime/

Universities: If you plan on renting out the property, selecting an area that has a nearby university can be very beneficial.

There are out-of-town students who prefer to NOT live on campus, and therefore, they need some other place to stay.

Property

After the location has been scouted and it has met the criteria for selection, it's time to zoom in and focus on the actual property itself.

Knowing what to look for in a property will partially depend on whether it is going to be used as a flip or a rental.

If the property is going to be used as a rental, it's important to pay attention to utilities and maintenance costs, such as:

• Trash pickup

- HOA fees

- Water service

If you are acquiring the property from another investor who has been renting it out, ask him or her about the rental history. This will give you a good idea of what you can expect to earn.

If the property is going to be purchased with the intention of flipping it for a profit, it makes sense to buy one in a high-demand area that is in need of a remodel.

If it's in excellent condition, it will be very expensive for the investor to buy. If it's in very poor condition, it will be very expensive for the investor to repair.

A property that offers a happy middle ground between extremely high price and extremely high repair and remodeling costs should be sought.

Ideally, there should be just enough wrong with the property to only require basic updating or remodeling, such as:

- Landscaping

- Repainting walls and ceilings

- New kitchen cabinets and flooring

If there are issues with the property's core, such as electrical, those types of repairs could be more costly than the return on investment when it comes time to sell.

The idea is to look for minor remodeling opportunities that can yield major returns on investment. The next chapter will provide some more depth on this topic.

Types of Property Upgrades that Produce the Biggest Returns

As real estate investors gain experience in the market, they will often tend to notice what works and what doesn't.

Some of them might learn the hard way that putting a large amount of money into remodeling a property doesn't always pay off the way they hoped it would.

Buyers might not appreciate certain remodeling efforts as much as the investor did.

But when studying the history of real estate and home improvement, certain patterns can be identified.

Looking for low-cost/high reward scenarios is what investors should try to look for. Of course, "low cost" doesn't necessarily mean "inexpensive." But if a $20,000 investment can lead to a $10,000 profit, that's a 50% return, which is very good.

Instead of simply looking at percentages, the cost must also be taken into consideration. A 100% return on a $3,000 investment will generate less money than a 50% return on a $20,000 investment. The high return from the $3,000 investment wouldn't mean much compared to the lower return of the $20,000 investment in this case.

Touching up a paint job might not add as much value to a house as remodeling an entire basement. But if you are able to do it yourself in a relatively short amount of time, it could be worthwhile.

Cost, amount of work involved, and percentages of returns should all be factored in when you are figuring the profit potential.

Here is a list of the remodeling projects that are known to have the highest returns on investment:

Completely finished basements

Cost – Very High

Amount of work involved – High

Return % - Moderate

Overall profit potential – Excellent

Garage Door Replacement

Cost – Moderate to High

Amount of work involved – Moderate

Return % - Very High

Overall profit potential - Good

Hardwood floors

Cost – Low to Moderate

Amount of work involved – Low to Moderate

Return Percentage – Very High

Overall profit potential - Good

Kitchen cabinets

Cost – Moderate

Amount of work involved – Moderate

Return % - Moderate to High

Overall profit potential - Fair

Landscaping

Cost – Moderate

Amount of work involved – Moderate

Return % - Very High

Overall profit potential - Good

Neutral wall paint colors

Cost- Low

Amount of work involved – Low

Return % - Moderate

Overall profit potential - Fair

Replacing the roof

Cost – Moderate

Amount of work involved – Moderate to High

Return Percentage – Excellent

Overall profit potential – Good

* * *

The exact numbers for these different types of remodeling projects will vary depending on the location and type of property. But regardless of the location and property, they are generally known to be worthwhile endeavors.

How to Make an Offer on a Property

Making an offer on a property doesn't just involve meeting the asking price. It involves the asking price and what other prospective buyers are offering to pay.

Be prepared to provide proof that you will be able to pay the asking price for the property.

Getting pre-approved is also recommended if you plan on taking out a loan.

Additionally, to show the seller that you're serious about buying the property, you might need to put down as much as 10% of the asking price upon the submission of your offer.

Working with a real estate agent can provide clarity as you go through the process step by step, so not everything has to be memorized beforehand.

Timing

Timing can be critical, particularly if you are seeking property in an area that has a small supply of properties available for sale.

If you find something good, don't try to wait for something even better. If you find a property that meets your criteria, place an offer.

When you tell your agent that you are ready to place an offer, the agent will likely call the seller's agent and ask if there are any other offers on the property.

Amount

Determining a realistic offer amount will depend on your ability to assess:

- the property value

- the amount of renovation that will need to be completed

- how outdated it is

- proximity to amenities

- what it has to offer (smart home, steel doors, central ac, etc)

Do your research on what similar properties in the area are going for and make sure that the one you're looking at isn't out of line with the rest of them.

If the property is significantly more expensive than others in the area, even though it is approximately the same size, find out why it's more expensive.

There might be something you are missing.

Is it only a half block away from the park?

Is it free of HOA fees in an area where most of the properties do have those fees?

Are the major systems and appliances (such as HVAC) more modern than what many of the other sellers in the area have?

After your agent gives you the formal offer to sign, he or she will submit it to the seller's agent. A response from the seller can be expected within 24 hours, although sometimes it will take longer.

If the offer is accepted, the next step will be closing.

How to Select Potentially Good Tenants

Whether you are renting out an apartment unit, a duplex, or a single-family house, selecting quality tenants is paramount.

Tenants can mean the difference between helping you pay your bills or having costly repairs to undergo.

Employment and Living History

• When setting up an application, make sure that it addresses the prospective tenant's employment history and prior addresses. If the person lacks stability, he or she might be a bigger risk.

Income

• Most home lenders (for houses and apartments) have a standard 3:1 ratio when it comes to income and rent.

The tenant should not be renting something that costs more than a third of their income.

If you are charging $1,000 a month for rent, the tenant should make an average of at least $3,000 a month consistently.

• Ask them to bring you copies of their pay stubs, and make sure they are for the past twelve months. If it is February, and you have a retail employee only bring you pay stubs that cover the past few months, the numbers can be misleading due to Black Friday and Christmas, since sales can get a boost around these times of year. A construction worker might get the bulk of his working hours in the spring and summer seasons.

The pay stubs should be fairly recent and cover all four seasons.

Credit

- Run a credit check on the prospective tenant. Having a high income will not mean much if the person is in a massive amount of debt on a regular basis.

- Get the prospective tenant's permission to run a credit check. Don't accept a credit report that the prospective tenant offers to bring you, as this comes with the possibility that the information was altered.

One website that offers credit checks for tenants is experian. But there are other websites available, as well.

Criminal Background Check

- Obtain the prospective tenant's name and date of birth to obtain a criminal background check.

- If a crime shows up in the report, it shouldn't immediately be a disqualification. In fact, some areas have laws in place to defend prospective tenants in those types of circumstances.

Pay attention to the crime's severity, frequency, relevancy, and the state of how recent it was. A person who got a speeding ticket fifteen years ago creates a much different scenario than a person who is a repeated offender of violent crime.

The criminal background check can typically be combined with the credit background check, depending on which company you use.

Punctuality

- If the prospective tenant shows up late the first time you meet him or her, that can be a warning sign of late payments in the future.

How to Make Real Estate Investing More Passive

Having a passive income stream can certainly be nice. Instead of having to work constantly, some initial setup work is done, and then the business runs without your active participation.

Although it might not be possible to make real estate investing entirely passive, it can certainly be made to be more passive than active.

In order to have the business run without your active participation, you have the option of hiring help.

This can be done by hiring a property manager.

Hiring a property manager to handle the monthly rental collection and daily maintenance routine can make things considerably more passive for the investor.

Some of them might even have connections and can help market your real estate business.

When the hiring process is in session, it's important to ask good questions that will help you make good decisions.

Try to find out:

• Length of time it usually takes for the manager to get a vacant unit filled

• Size of the manager's staff

• How many units the manager is currently managing

• Whether the manager has evicted anyone before, and if so, how he or she handled it

• What his or her process consists of when it comes to applicant screening

Make your objectives and expectations clear. You will need to decide how active or passive you'd like to be.

If you'd like your real estate rental business to be as passive as possible, make it clear to the prospective property manager that he or she will be expected to do the entire process from start to finish.

This can include, but is not limited to:

• hiring contractors

• photographing the property to prepare it for advertising

• marketing the property

• screening applicants

• collecting rent

• handling all of the maintenance

• showing the property

• taking care of late payments and enforcing late fees when necessary

• performing inspections regularly

• assemble annual reports and tax documentation

• keeping you updated about the condition of the property

When it comes time to go through the property management contract, take notice of anything that presents a problem for you and ask if they would be willing to be flexible about it.

How to Invest in Real Estate without Having to Manage Tenants, Hire Property Managers, or Maintain Physical Property

To invest in real estate without dealing with the drawbacks that owning physical property and managing tenants have, there is the option of investing in Real Estate Investment Trusts (REITs) by buying shares in the stock market.

Real Estate Investment Trusts are companies that own properties that produce income. Shares can be purchased from an online broker.

Since different online brokerages have different pros and cons, it's important to choose one that is right for your particular situation.

This chapter will cover some of the most popular online brokers, as well as the pros and cons to each one, how much money they charge per trade via commissions, and what the minimum account balance must be.

Note: Brokers can change their rule structure at anytime, so it's important to visit their websites to verify that the information is current.

E*TRADE

This broker is among the most popular. It was founded in 1982, and their first online trade took place in 1983. They are headquartered in New York City with 30 retail branches across the United States.

Commission fees per trade: $6.95, but only $4.95 with 30 or more trades per quarter

Commission fees for mutual funds: $19.99

Account minimum: $500

Pros

• The platform is known to be beginner-friendly and easy to use

• Offers personalized support and guidance

• Offers independent analyst research

• Has investing tools

• Reduced commission fees for traders who place more than 30 trades per quarter

• Their mobile app makes them more accessible

• Stocks, bonds, options, ETFs, and mutual funds are all available as investment choices

Cons

• There are other brokers that offer smaller commission fees

• There are other brokers that do not require a minimum account balance

Ally

Ally Invest seems to offer a good balance between beginner-friendly and advanced. It's good for beginner investors because there is no minimum account balance required to get started, while the more advanced investor might appreciate their charting, data, and analytical tools.

There are no inactivity fees if the account remains dormant for a while.

Commission fees per trade: $4.95, but only $3.95 with 30 or more trades per quarter

Commission fees for mutual funds: $9.95

Account minimum: $0

Pros

- Lower commission fees than many other brokers

- No minimum account balance requirement

- Customer service is available 24/7

- Tools and informational articles available

- SIPC covered, so up to $250,000 worth of cash funds are protected if *Ally Invest* fails

- Stocks, bonds, options, ETFs, commission-free ETFs, margin accounts, and mutual funds are all available as investment choices

- Offers FOREX trading

- Offers automated portfolio management

Cons

• They do not offer zero-fee transaction for mutual funds

Merrill Edge

Bank of America is their parent company.

Commission fees per trade: $6.95

Account minimum: $0

Pros

• No minimum account balance required

• Customer service available 24/7

• Access to award-winning research

• Has tools that help you make more informed investment decisions

• Stocks, bonds, options, ETFs, mutual funds or professionally managed portfolios are all available as investment choices

• Offers *Market Pro* for active investors

Cons

• There are other brokers that offer cheaper commission fees.

• To qualify for ten $0 online stock and ETF trades per month (the most basic tier), a three-month average balance of at least

$20,000 between Bank of America and Merrill Edge accounts must be maintained, which many people might find unrealistic.

AMERITRADE

This brokerage has over 360 branches in the United States.

Commission fees per trade: $6.95

Account minimum: $0

Pros

- No minimum account balance required

- Includes many advanced features

- Investment selection includes equities, options, futures, and FOREX

- Offers personalized coaching via social media, webcasts, and in-person workshops

- Allows the users to "paper trade" for practice without risking real money

- Customer service available 24/7

Cons

- There are other brokers that offer cheaper commission fees.

- Broker-assisted fees are $44.99, which some investors might find expensive.

Fidelity

They used to have an account minimum requirement for mutual funds, but they have now done away with that. They have zero expense ratio for index funds.

Commission fees per trade: $4.95

Account minimum: $0

Pros

- Offers help with planning for retirement and advice on wealth management
- Robust investing tools
- No minimum amount of money required to open an account
- Zero expense ratio index funds
- Zero minimum investment mutual funds
- Customer service available 24/7
- Lower commission fees than many other brokers
- Covered by FDIC and SIPC

Cons

- Need to deposit $50,000-$99,000 to qualify for their promotional offer of 300 free trades over a 2 year period, which some people may find to be too much money.

* * *

If you are feeling indecisive about which online broker to use, know that there is no commitment involved. If you find another broker later on that fits your needs better, you can always switch over.

Closing

Whether you'd like to invest in commercial real estate, duplexes, single-family homes, or apartments, the core principals remain generally the same—looking out for opportunities and buying property in high-demand areas.

Some of the methods are more passive than others, but they all have the potential to be profitable for the investor.

Being a successful real estate investor might not be easy, but it shouldn't have to be scary.

Investors are essentially trying to put their money to work for them. Although the concepts of real estate investing might be rather straight forward, they can be challenging to actually put into practice.

Managing risk and understanding economics can give you an edge in the market, but the knowledge that comes from experience can be even better.

More from D.K. Livingston

Investing in Dividend Stocks for Beginners, available at all *Amazon* stores, including U.S.

How to Read Stock Charts, available at all *Amazon* stores, including U.S.

www.ingramcontent.com/pod-product-compliance
Lightning Source LLC
Chambersburg PA
CBHW030738180526
45157CB00008BA/3219